Intellectual Disability

 caring for yourself and others

Living and caring as God intends.
Sharing in the *Imago Dei.*
A place for everyBody's glory.

PASTORAL · OUTREACH · SERIES ·

Intellectual
Disability

caring for yourself and others

Cristina Gangemi
Liam Waldron

redemptorist
p u b l i c a t i o n s

Published by Redemptorist Publications
Alphonsus House, Chawton, Hampshire, GU34 3HQ, UK
Tel: +44 (0)1420 88222, Fax: +44 (0)1420 88805
Email: rp@rpbooks.co.uk, www.rpbooks.co.uk

A registered charity limited by guarantee
Registered in England 3261721

Series Editor: Sister Janet Fearns
Edited by Mandy Woods
Designed by Eliana Thompson

ISBN 978-0-85231-515-6

A CIP catalogue record for this book is available from the British Library.
The author would like to thank all those who have contributed to this book with their
true stories.

The publisher gratefully acknowledges permission to use the following copyright material:
Excerpts from the New Revised Standard Version Bible: Anglicised Edition, © 1989, 1995,
Division of Christian Education of the National Council of the Churches of Christ in the
United States of America. Used by permission. All rights reserved.

Every effort has been made to trace copyright holders and to obtain their permission for the
use of copyright material. The publisher apologises for any errors or omissions and would be
grateful for notification of any corrections that should be incorporated in future reprints or
editions of this book.

Printed by Lithgo Press Ltd.,
Leicester, LE8 6NU

Introduction: who is welcomed?

Can you look back over your lives and ministries and ask yourself how many intellectually disabled people have been among your parishioners? How many people who live with diverse ways of learning and experiencing the world have been welcomed or have had access to pastoral care?

Who has been enabled and who has been disabled?

When we think of what it means to be a balanced society and a welcoming parish community we may realise it is rare that people who have been disabled are re-membered.

A community is often presumed to be made up of people who all have the same way of acting, communicating and thinking. Certainly our buildings, architecture and resources reflect this. But why is this so?

If the Christian community is called to be a place for all to find and know God, why are so many disabled people still missing from our communities, especially as their stories bring the joy of diversity and creativity to the world?

After all, as Pope Francis says, "a world where everyone is the same would be a boring world" (Pope Francis, 2016). Indeed, as people, we are most definitely all equal in the fact that we are all different.

Since the closing of institutions which formerly housed people who were intellectually and physically disabled, a key stated priority of Western governments and health services has been the placement and integration of people with disabilities in the community. Institutional care has instead become community care.

All services for people with disabilities, be they related to housing, healthcare or employment, are underpinned by legislation. These are shaped by the work of the disability rights movement, marked by an emphasis on inclusion, equality and choice.

Much progress has been made towards the improvement of the lives of people with disabilities. The outmoded "medical model" of disability has been replaced by the "social model" which, while also coming under scrutiny from some quarters, sees wider society as that which limits the ability of people with disabilities to live their lives to the full. Through that lens, people with a disability are defined not by what they cannot do based on a medical diagnosis, but rather by what they can do in the right circumstances. It is not the "disability" which disables but rather the attitude of the wider population.

The drive for disability equality, then, emerges from the social model of disability. It seeks to generally reduce, in terms of opportunity and treatment, the differences between carer and client and between disabled people and non-disabled people.

Equality requires a high level of collaboration between all in society to ensure that no person is treated unfairly due to the presence of a disability. This collaboration is not left to chance and is now shaped by policy and legislation.

Despite progress, reports continue to highlight not only instances of illegal discrimination, but also worryingly high levels of social isolation and loneliness among people with disabilities.

Research shows that social isolation and loneliness are significant problems in our society, which both cause both mental and physical ill-health, and also frequently result from it.

Many people with disabilities who already experience challenges in making and maintaining friendships are at a particular risk of falling into social isolation and loneliness.

Living in the community, even with the force of legal protection on their side, does not guarantee social acceptance or the formation of life-giving caring relationships.

It seems, then, that the sort of caring friendships which can reduce the effects of isolation and loneliness must be freely given and accepted and require both commitment and a recognition of the worth of "the other", irrespective of ability.

This book will take you on a reflective journey. We invite you to explore the lives of disabled people within history and how their life and faith have been organised for them rather than with them.

Chapter 1 explores the personhood of people with disabilities and the language that is used to enable or disable their lives.

In Chapter 2, we will gain an understanding of the theology of disability which prompts us to reflect on why it is we care about our brothers and sisters with disabilities.

Chapter 3 will consider how we can care for our brothers and sisters with intellectual disabilities, while Chapter 4 considers one of the consequences of not caring – namely, the problems of isolation and loneliness which are a reality for many with an intellectual disability.

Having considered these important issues, Chapter 5 will look at spirituality and storytelling and how Christ's ministry and approach can guide the way that care is given. This method will, we hope, contribute to the fostering of communities of belonging within faith communities.

Chapter 6 sets out some practical guidance for how you and your faith community can make the changes that are needed to enable people and to celebrate the richness of diversity found in the lives and stories of people who have been disabled.

Our conclusion will invite you, the reader, to be the catalyst for change and the respectful and empathic provider of care.

Some of the chapters provide activities for you to undertake, alone or with your faith community, so that together, as agents of evangelisation, you may foster communities where all people know and experience that they belong. This book will, therefore, be a resource for you and your community so that, together, we can ensure that our practice and resources enable creative spaces for people's stories to be told and embraced, both in times of joy and in times of sadness.

1

"I am": understanding personhood and disability

The importance of language

"Language holds an important place in how the lives and stories of people are shared and discussed" (*Living Fully (LF)* Statement 2016).

Negative language and a lack of access **disables** people, setting up "physical, cultural, and attitudinal barriers, which prevent people from living fully" (LF Statement 2016). Disabling factors (physical, intellectual and/or emotional) may be a part of someone's life, but "they are persons first" (Reinders, 2016).

Each and every person has God's given dignity by virtue of their creation. As one encounters *people* who have been disabled by the above disabling factors, it is a constant challenge to reject limiting labels, stereotypes and assumptions.

In this book we will spend time thinking about issues that impact the lives and care of people who have been intellectually disabled. We therefore invite each reader to "examine their own opinions and language" (LF Statement 2016), asking themselves how they can *en*able people rather than *dis*able them.

You might be wondering why we are using the term *intellectual disability*, as it is sometimes referred to as "learning disability", so let us stop and think about this a little more.

Please spend just a few minutes examining your own language and opinions and the way in which they may, perhaps unwittingly, contribute to the social isolation and diminished expectations of a person named Juliette.

Personal reflection:

Juliette is an 18-year-old young woman who was born with a medical condition that had direct outcomes for how her brain functioned and how it sent messages to the rest of her body. Juliette was born on the spectrum of autism. In her case, this meant that she had no formal speech and her way of learning needed creative images, sign language and sensory activities. Juliette has always been told she has a "learning difficulty".

1. Take five minutes and ask yourself what the first images and words are that come to your mind when you see or hear the term
   Learning Difficulty/Disability

2. Write down or record your reactions

3. What do you notice about the images and words you have encountered?

Generally, people tend to associate negative words and images with the phrases "learning difficulty" and "learning disability", explaining *learning difficulty* in such terms as "not being able to read, having problems with learning, can't write, disabled" and many more.

Such negative views influence our attitudes regarding the ability of others, leading us to emphasise what people *cannot* do rather than what they *can* do.

The experience of one of the authors, however, has been the very opposite of this. She worked for many years in a special needs school for young people with disabilities. The school was a place where the students were enabled to learn in many creative ways. Far from having *learning difficulties*, they were, indeed, very *creative learners*.

Why is this act of God so important in Juliette's story?

We have heard how Juliette lives on the spectrum of autism and that she is a "creative learner". If, when being taught, Juliette was only provided with books filled with copious text and expected to write all that she learned, we would find that she was being set intellectual tasks that present boundaries to her creativity. The teaching methods and intellectual resources used would not positively facilitate the creative way in which she learns.

The use of creative and imaginative teaching methods and resources that suit the manner in which Juliette learns would allow her to overcome the obstacles that more traditional teaching methods can sometimes place before a learner like Juliette. Approaches which respond to Juliette's own way of learning would reveal her God–given creativity and enable her to achieve according to her own abilities and interests.

Juliette's story helps us to recognise that people learn differently, that on recognising this, we have to adapt, and that if we adapt, then we will find that people with intellectual disabilities have a huge range of capabilities that are in danger of going unrecognised. Juliette, like each of us, is, in the words of the psalmist, "fearfully and wonderfully made" (Psalm 139:14), and when we all work together creatively, this mystery is more clearly revealed to us.

Language, as we can see, has a very profound impact on the life story of a person, no matter what their perceived ability might be.

If we are asking ourselves questions about the language we use, we have to also ask if our perceptions, attitudes and activities serve to create a world where all people belong.

When we feel rejected, and that we do not belong, we are moved to question our own purpose in the world. Without a strong sense of "belonging", we come to feel worthless. Jesus came into the world that we might all have life in its fullness, but when we feel that we do not belong, our lives are less than full.

But why are some people consigned to this life of isolation?

Why are people "dis-abled"?

The quest to understand "what it means to be human" (Jones, 2004) has been at the forefront of human discovery and conversation for thousands of years. Throughout history, philosophers such as Plato, Aristotle, Descartes and many more have undertaken intense thinking and discussion around the subject.

Is a person a person because of their bodily movements?
How should a body look? Who decides how the body should look?
Is personhood about the way people walk, or do not walk? Is it because of a body shape or because of a person's intellect? What is intellect? Is a human person a body *and* a spirit or a fusion of body with spirit? Whose life is valuable and whose life is not?
So many questions!

As history has unfolded, classicism has had a profound effect upon how the human person is defined. The classical image of a body has to conform to the recognised standard set by the ancient Greeks and Romans. Their concept of being fully human was found in a typical shape and way of doing things. If the person did not conform to this standard, they were thought to be weak and therefore risked rejection.

This approach has meant that a particular model of humanity has influenced centuries of culture. People have been judged negatively if their body is not classical. They have not been recognised for the wonder of who they are.

Based on Psalm 139:14

More often than not, this approach to the human person has served only to imprison and *dis*-able bodies. Hierarchies of abilities have emerged. A culture of them and us has been *created* within the human story and has, somehow, rippled into the Christian story as well. One only has to look at much Christian art, designed to teach people about faith, to notice that strength is often presented though the classical body while weakness and sin are often presented by a body that does not conform to the set standard. This has added to the unspoken culture of them and us.

Please take fifteen minutes, alone or with a group, to discuss the following, or to reflect alone on it:

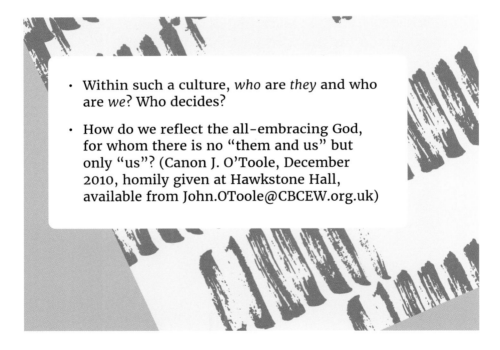

- Within such a culture, *who* are *they* and who are *we*? Who decides?

- How do we reflect the all-embracing God, for whom there is no "them and us" but only "us"? (Canon J. O'Toole, December 2010, homily given at Hawkstone Hall, available from John.OToole@CBCEW.org.uk)

In a Church and culture where the concept of "them and us" is removed, we *all* accept that we *all* belong, and people are *enabled*. The barriers that exclude people just would *not* exist and we would be able to meet each other, recognising our valued place *within* the "Image of God" and *as* the Image of God. Though no person should be excluded from our communities of belonging, unfortunately many are.

In the following chapters, we will explore the *Imago Dei* (Image of God) and its relevance in the lives of people who have been intellectually disabled, as well as exploring the devastating effects of exclusion, often taking the form of depression, isolation and loneliness.

2

Disability theology and why we care for each other

Disability theology has been described as the attempt to understand God and the Christian Gospel against the background of the experiences of people with disabilities (Swinton, 2010). It asks theological questions about what it means to have a disability, or to encounter those with a disability, and prompts us to consider these questions from a faith perspective. It invites us to open our hearts to the diversity in God's creation and to consider the proper and faithful response to the Christian challenge to care for all our brothers and sisters, including people with disabilities.

Reflecting on the mutual care that people with and without disability show for each other raises questions regarding the origin, nature and meaning of "being human".

Answers to these questions come from an understanding of God as creator of humankind and of the consequences of this for the meaning and shape of the relationship between human persons.

Intellectual disability and the problem of loneliness prompt us to focus on the nature of human relationships, not only in theory but also in practice.

The human love of neighbour is the reflection of the love of God for all, and human activity takes place against a background of the eternal, which is God.

In attempting to address the many challenges our brothers and sisters with disabilities face and in understanding how we can care for each other in an authentic way, we need to try to understand what it means to be human in the eyes of God who created us, God's desire for his creation and how we should respond to the mystery that we are God's people.

Our reflections on and understanding of the nature of the human person and on human relations more generally make a difference to our brothers and sisters with disabilities. As the theologian Jürgen Moltmann comments,

> "Our knowledge of the stars is a matter of indifference to the stars themselves, but our knowledge of man is not without consequences for the very being of man. It is a knowledge which itself alters man."

Moltmann, 1974, pp. x–xi

The Imago Dei – the Image of God

We read in the Book of Genesis that it is God who creates all new things and when humanity acknowledges God as "Creator", it thereby acknowledges itself as "created" and therefore recognises the "claim" that God has on us, his creatures.

Genesis says that after creating each thing, God affirmed what he had created as "good" and it was good because God had created it.

We see all around us the rich diversity in God's creation – a world and a people created for God and for each other. God's image is on each one of us.

As "creatures", having been created by God, we are not left to make our own way but, rather, are created for an ongoing relationship with God and with each other.

All "creatures", no matter what their ability is, are intimately related to God and called into relationship with God, though the way each of us acknowledges this and responds to God can differ.

God, as the creator of humankind, is therefore in a loving relationship with us which forms the basis of our relationship with each other.

As creatures of a loving God, we have the image of our creator – an *Imago Dei*. Genesis 1:26 tells us that God said, "Let us make humankind in our image, according to our likeness; and let them have dominion over the fish of the sea, and over the birds of the air, and over the cattle, and over all the wild animals of the earth, and over every creeping thing that creeps upon the earth."

Later, the Gospels introduce another element to the claim that we are made in God's "image and likeness":

We have Jesus Christ, true God and true man, who is the image of God and who is the one we are called to be "like".

The theologian Kathryn Tanner understands the meaning of the *Imago Dei* as key to understanding the personal relations we have with others, be they people with disabilities or not, and the dignity with which we should treat each other. She comments,

> "Creation is a way of pointing out a special relation between them [humankind] and God. Human beings gain their unique dignity, not by virtue of anything they possess in and of themselves, but by being God's image – by reflecting, corresponding to, following obediently after, making an appropriate response to, the God who has created them for such a relationship."

Tanner, 1993, p. 572

Being created in God's image, therefore, is not only a one-off event, but is also a journey in which we become more Christ-like, reaching out the hand of loving friendship to those who are isolated, lonely and rejected.

If we are created to be in caring relationships with others, then the problem of friendlessness and loneliness in our society, for example, must be an indication that we are falling short in living out our vocation – that we are not the caring brothers and sisters we are created to be.

15

The existence of lonely people with intellectual disabilities in our world is a sign of broken relationships.

When humanity ignores the cry of loneliness of people with intellectual disabilities, it is ignoring its true nature as *Imago Dei*, as it is refusing to express the love Christ showed for those who were forgotten and rejected, and rejecting its vocation to care for others.

As brothers and sisters of each other, we are in communion with one another

As creatures of the creator God, sharing his image, we are "in communion" with one another. While "communion" is a word that has many meanings – for example, it is used to describe the Eucharist itself – it also refers to a form of "being together" at a deep level, where those "in communion" with each other are more than mere acquaintances, or even more than "friends". They care about each other at a fundamental level to the extent that one does not live life in its fullness without caring for and being "in communion" with others.

The Gospel stories of those whom Jesus encountered with disabilities tell of their marginalisation and rejection by their own communities. They were not "in communion" with others.

Living in communion with others requires a fundamental change of heart by us all and a turning to "the other" as another "self" in order to develop a bond where the joys and sorrows of one become the joys and sorrows of the other.

For Christians, this bond between people with and without disabilities is founded on a bond of communion with Christ. It is much more than a loose association with others.

As Christians, we are invited to care for others and to be witnesses to the living out of "communion" in our own lives.

"Communion" is about being "with" the other as well as being "for" the other. It recognises the commonality between "carer" and "cared for". It emphasises the point that without each other, none of us, no matter what our ability is, can hope to live life to the full, as God intended.

When God's people are truly "in communion" with one another, they are compelled to embrace each other and to be true to their calling as persons who love others irrespective of perceived abilities.

A pastoral approach to the care of people with intellectual disabilities by church communities does need to be underpinned by a vision that seeks the fullness of life for all. As Volf comments,

> "at the heart of every good theology lies, not simply a plausible intellectual vision, but, more importantly, a compelling account of a way of life".

Volf, 2002, p. 247

3

How can we care?

In our society, the care of our brothers and sisters with intellectual disabilities is provided by family, voluntary bodies, church organisations, local authorities and also governmental agencies which focus on the provision of housing, healthcare, education and training. However, many people with intellectual disabilities continue to find themselves isolated, lonely and forgotten.

The continued presence of lonely people in our communities is a challenge to the providers of services to people with intellectual disabilities, though the kinds of friendships that we all want and need to thrive are not easily legislated for. Indeed, as Gillibrand (2010, p. 180) comments insightfully, "there are things which cannot be contained within the constraints of any legal system, which are love and care themselves".

Challenging the Church to care

The care provided by church communities can also fall short. Occasionally there can be a tendency to treat the care of those who are disadvantaged, including people with disabilities, as one pastoral priority among other competing priorities, or as the responsibility of an appointed pastoral committee, for example. Rather, the care of people with disabilities is integral to what it means to be "Church" in the first place.

The practices of friendship and hospitality as understood from the standpoint of Christian theology can address some of the difficulties faced by our brothers and sisters with disabilities, including the problem of loneliness, but they must permeate the entire life of the Church.

Opportunities need to be created in our churches and parishes for the fostering of the sort of life-giving friendships that bring joy and hope. For as long as the difficulties faced by people with intellectual disabilities are treated merely as an "issue", without the realisation that no life is complete while the lives of others are incomplete, the problem of loneliness will never be adequately addressed.

Caring is a risky business

We may be disappointed that occasionally churches, voluntary bodies and state agencies fail to care adequately for people with disabilities.

What is needed is a response that arises out of a dialogue between all the contributors – including people with disabilities themselves and their families and supporters – to the discussion regarding what constitutes the good life for people with intellectual disabilities.

Conversations between all interested parties – political, legislative and church-based – should continue so that solutions to the many challenges faced by people with disabilities can be explored.

The problems of loneliness and social isolation in particular are urgent, requiring not only innovation in designing pastoral programmes (that include input from people with disabilities themselves) that could address these issues, but also generosity and selflessness on the part of those who seek to care for our brothers and sisters with disabilities.

The call to care for others through the practice of Christian friendship and hospitality is a radical call. Real friendships between people are not based solely on the fact that they have things in common. Rather, true authentic friendship has something of the mystery of God about it.

Fostering authentic friendships with people with intellectual disabilities, or indeed with anyone, involves a risk: we find that we must surrender our status as we encounter the other as brother or sister. It acknowledges that our differences, while present, are not that important and we reach a point where, as Catholic philosopher, theologian and humanitarian Jean Vanier puts it, we do not know who is helping whom.

Though risky, caring for our brothers and sisters with intellectual disabilities can begin with simple gestures.

The American theologian Sharon Kugler, writing of her experience as a chaplain, comments that it is in caring for people in surprising ways, through performing small and seemingly insignificant loving gestures, that we are often most effective (Kugler, 2013).

This echoes that often-quoted phrase of St Teresa of Calcutta –

> "Not all of us can do great things. But we can do small things with great love."

These "small things" can be welcome starting points for addressing issues of loneliness and isolation among our brothers and sisters with intellectual disabilities. In their practice, as we care for others, we encounter the "God of the everyday" who cares for and loves each of us regardless of ability.

And yet, doing something "for" others is only the start of our reaching out. As Jean Vanier comments,

> "In the end, the most important thing is not to do things for people who are poor and in distress, but to enter into relationship with them, to be with them and help them find confidence in themselves and discover their own gifts."

> *Vanier, 1989, p.142*

When we really care, we are reminded of the bond that unites us as brothers and sisters of each other, where, together, as children of a common Father, we can share our stories and live fully the life we have been gifted.

4

What happens when we don't care?

Isolation and loneliness

Loneliness and isolation are complex phenomena with medical, psychological, sociological, political, spiritual and theological dimensions. When identifying someone as "isolated", for example, we observe that a person's life is missing particular social relationships that result in this "isolation".

Isolation can be the result of alienation experienced as a societal response to "difference", be that difference based on culture, language or disability.

Isolation and loneliness are concerned with the quality of human relationships and the level of the authenticity of these relationships with the "other" over time, and with the emotional, psychological and spiritual consequences of the lack of life-giving relationships.

The long-term experience of enforced social isolation and resulting loneliness can have devastating consequences for those who experience it. Not only is isolation both a cause and an effect of mental ill health, it also has real, measurable, damaging physiological effects, thereby causing other illness and ultimately shortening life.

Isolation and loneliness: the fate of many with an intellectual disability

Isolation and loneliness are the sad experiences of many of our brothers and sisters with intellectual disabilities and can be a difficult problem to tackle.

Some with intellectual disabilities may have difficulty expressing their feelings and opinions verbally, although there are, of course, many other means by which they can reveal their stories to us and we can reveal ours to them.

Spoken words are not always necessary – pictures, gestures, signs and symbols are all used to tell a story. The inability or even unwillingness of those who care for people with intellectual disabilities to appreciate the story being told, however, leads to a missed opportunity to learn about the importance of friends and friendship.

Without open hearts and minds, and without a resolve to pay respectful attention, we might never understand the challenge of social isolation and loneliness that is part of the lives of so many with disabilities. We too miss out – on the chance to tell our own story to others for whom we care, and on the opportunity to open ourselves to the possibility of a life-giving friendship with a person with disability.

Not all people with disabilities are lonely. Many lead full and happy lives with good social connections and supportive friendships. They experience the love of those who care for them in their families, neighbourhoods and perhaps churches and parishes of which they are part.

The increased presence of people with intellectual disabilities in our neighbourhoods and workplaces as a result of the closure of institutions may give the appearance of a uniformly content disabled population living lives like any other.

But the simple presence in the community of people with intellectual disabilities is not an indication of their acceptance by that community, or of their acceptance to the extent that they would ever be considered as potential friends for those without disabilities, for example.

That many people with intellectual disability now live independently or go to work daily does not mean that they have friends or that they are not lonely.

Research into the life experiences of people with intellectual disabilities highlights the difficulties they often experience when trying to initiate the kinds of interpersonal relationships and friendships that could alleviate the effects of isolation. Similar difficulties are also often experienced in responding to offers of friendship and in sustaining friendships.

In general, children with intellectual disabilities often experience rejection in their attempts to form friendships. Their loneliness has been linked directly to a limited social network and to frequent rejection by their peers. They may not display the increasing independence that comes with growing up into adolescence.

The difficulties faced by children and adolescents with intellectual disabilities in forming and maintaining friendships may only worsen as they grow up. According to Bigby (2004, p. 121), the formation of friendships becomes even more difficult as they outlive their parents and experience a "shrinkage of their social networks".

Likewise, Mencap's 2016 report on friendships and socialising among people with an intellectual disability states that such people are vulnerable to experiencing loneliness as they are likely to have smaller social networks and fewer friends than those without a disability.

This problem, the report goes on to say, begins in childhood, when children with a disability tend to have weaker social relationships than others and find making friends difficult (Mencap, 2016). It reveals the shocking finding that while fifteen to thirty per cent of the general population experience chronic loneliness, that figure is fifty per cent for those with an intellectual disability.

Research not only tells us that people with intellectual disabilities are lonely, it also reveals why they might be lonely, thereby opening up avenues of investigation for addressing the problem.

Some of these relate to the type of schooling that people with disabilities receive, the level of formal education they attain, their employment status, their income level, their housing situation and their state of health. Unfortunately, many people with disabilities do not "score" highly in these areas.

As a result, many people with intellectual disabilities are among us yet "invisible". Many are part of our neighbourhoods and workplaces but are not part of our lives.

Using an "iceberg" analogy, Cacioppo comments:

> "Civic engagement is the chunk of ice we see floating above the surface. Below the water line lurks the much deeper issue of individual feelings of isolation. If civic engagement is to contribute substantially to assuaging the problem of loneliness, then it cannot be something merely akin to networking at a trade show. What individuals need is meaningful connection, not superficial glad handling."
>
> *Cacioppo and Patrick, 2008, p. 26*

This reminds us that a high level of visibility of people with intellectual disabilities is no guarantee of a satisfactory level of interpersonal relationships.

People with intellectual disabilities have been clear about the solution to their loneliness. The solution is friendship that is authentic and emotionally healthy and that continues to develop over time.

It is the absence of such friendships that renders the person with an intellectual disability lonely. A lonely life cannot be said to be a life lived to the full.

Real authentic human interconnectedness is the only thing that can offer hope to lonely people and mute the effects of loneliness, but it can be difficult to achieve. Real friendship cannot be forced. It is not a project that can be planned with specifically measurable outcomes.

The Christian vision of humankind challenges each one of us to be "brother" and "sister" to each other, as authentically as necessary to address the problems of isolation and loneliness.

This vision understands God as the loving creator of each person in God's own image, which, in turn, renders each of us a brother or sister to every other person.

In each of us is a "spark" of the divine. We are connected at such a deep level that when we reach out in loving friendship to another, we are imitating and reflecting the love that God has for us. While such an understanding of our profound connectedness is something to celebrate, it presents us with a challenge – namely, that we are called to care for each other through the practice of unselfish love in our daily interactions with others.

We are challenged to give and to love without expectation of being loved in the same way in return. We are all brothers and sisters of each other, irrespective of difference. In fostering life-giving relationships – the kind that can lift the heavy burden of sadness that results from loneliness – we together are being faithful to our purpose in God's creation.

5

Showing that we care: everyBody has a story

The previous chapters have looked at issues of personhood, theology, models of care, and loneliness and isolation – especially as experienced by people who have been intellectually disabled – and at the need for a new understanding of communion and the vocation that we all have towards and with one another.

Often, the only experience of friendship for people with intellectual disabilities comes from people who are paid to care for them.

The time has come for this to change and for new opportunities and models of care, built on a foundation of friendship and mutual care, to be explored, irrespective of ability.

Let us now reflect on the practical issue of care in the lives of people who have been intellectually disabled, so that we can identify the barriers that prevent the provision of this type of care and do our part in removing these barriers.

Intellectual disabilities, death and bereavement

In her powerful book *Loss and Learning Disability* (2003, p. 153), Noelle Blackman describes an unspoken anxiety that she has encountered in the many people with intellectual disabilities with whom she has worked: "Will anyone care when I die?" This was displayed especially in the words and actions of a young man named Alan. Blackman describes his fear as having roots in deep-seated loneliness, an experience of isolation and in the "voice of society that places little value on the life" of someone who has been intellectually disabled. "Will anyone care?" is a profound question for the whole of society, and certainly for the Church.

Theoretically, within the care system in the United Kingdom, a huge shift has taken place, one which has seen care directed by personalisation (enabling the person who is being cared for to make choices and decisions for themselves) and co-production (enabling their opinions, choices and decisions to be formative in the systems and services of the provider of their care) become the norm.

Both approaches to care are designed to promote the autonomy of people with intellectual disabilities and to enable them to live self-directed lives.

In spite of this, however, many people with disabilities continue to live friendless, lonely and isolated lives. Let us now take some time to think about this so that we might identify where changes need to be made so that true communion can be practised – the kind of communion that could address the problem of loneliness.

Take twenty minutes to reflect, alone or in a group, on the following questions. Please record your reflections.

1. Who are the people who care in the lives of people with intellectual disabilities?

2. How far does personalisation and co-production actually translate into practice?

3. Where, in your role in ministry or in a parish, do you experience "communion" with others?

4. How are people truly enabled to enjoy a life that is socially, physically and spiritually fulfilled?

5. How, in a practical way, can we live so that we acknowledge that each person is created in the *Imago Dei*, the Image of God?

One could be tempted to answer the first question by making a list of people and organisations.

If we are to be an enabling community in which there is no "them and us", the answer instead should be that *we must all care.*

If someone does not have a voice to speak with in their own life, and if they are not present in faith communities or if they are not able to live and narrate their own experiences of God, then everybody needs to care because "everyBody has a story" and every story matters (Gangemi et al., 2010).

"EveryBody Has a Story"

In 2010, thirty intellectually disabled people became research partners in a project that sought to "meet people with intellectual disabilities and respond to their spiritual and religious needs" (Gangemi et al., 2010).

The project team records that it was a time of revelation for all involved. All partners were creative learners and seemed, once given the space and creative tools to express themselves, to "have an urgency to narrate their story" (Gangemi et al., 2010), highlighting the importance of storytelling and self-expression in people's lives. Taking their lead, let us now look at *why* story matters so much and where we can find a model of care that brings fullness of life rather than a disabling story of rejection, exclusion and loneliness.

Recently, Dr Zach Duke, a brilliant and vibrant theologian, interviewed Jean Vanier, the founder of the L'Arche community, a worldwide organisation where people with and without disabilities live together. In this interview Jean shared much of his own journey as a disciple who has lived most of his life with people who have been intellectually disabled.

Zach shared with us how much he had learnt from Jean's story: how to spend time with people with intellectual disabilities; how these could become moments of "mutual relationships of friendship" (Badetti, 2016, p. 158). Zach discovered how to replace a concept of being a care provider with that of being drawn into profound experiences, where the very presence and creativity of each person revealed an "opportunity to meet, touch and feel the presence of God" (Duke and Vanier, 2017).

The language and experience of mutual transformation and relationship was very different to that of service provider and carer.

It is often in the experience of sharing a person's story that new learning and mutual recognition take place.

In the personal experience of one of the authors of this book (Cristina Gangemi), and more recently in her work within the Livability charity (Livability, 2017), she has noted the power of story and how spending time with people and sharing in their stories has enabled a very different type of care. When a carer feels that their role is about *doing* something *for* someone rather than *being with* someone, everything is turned into a chore... the model of care is functional.

However, when we undertake our roles as actors within the story of the person we have before us, everything takes on a new meaning. *Making* time to *spend* time with each other, we learn from one another and enjoy a creative space in which to communicate.

Through story, each person involved enters into each other's reality and colours each other's lives through the shared joys and challenges of life. It becomes a way to care that enjoys a mutual living out of a "celebration of diversity" (Pope Francis, 2016).

This model of care and story-gathering is nothing new. Indeed, in the lives of people who had been disabled the most powerful witness to such a model is Jesus.

The life and mission of Jesus gives examples of how to enter into the real-life stories of people, offering friendship and authentic love.

Story after story in the Gospels see Jesus as a meeting point, where he encouraged people to recognise the worth in each other. However, Jesus seemed to have a particular focus on meeting people whom some had decided were not as valuable as others.

Here we see Jesus challenging the culture of "them and us". In the document of the Second Vatican Council that focuses on the "Divine Word" (*Dei Verbum*) we are taught that the very purpose of Christ's body and mission was to invite us into the mystery and purpose of the incarnation:

> "Christ established on earth the kingdom of God, revealing his Father and himself through words and deeds... The invisible God, from the fullness of his love, addresses humankind as friends in order to invite them into his own company."

Dei Verbum, Second Vatican Council, 1965

The words and actions of Jesus, therefore, invite each and every person into friendship with God, and into an understanding of humanness that challenges us to love and value each other as equals. People who have been disabled are much like any other person in that they have stories, experiences, ideas, knowledge and emotions to share.

However, when someone's story is not fully acknowledged within models of care or in faith activities, such individuals live in danger of becoming "objects of pity and opportunities to grow in sanctification" (Masters, 2016).

Cristina Gangemi's own story of sharing her life with people who are intellectually disabled has been filled with very different experiences and moments of mutual transformation. It has been touched by the joys and vulnerabilities that we all face. She has noted that the lives and stories of disabled people "are as variable as any one person's is from another" (Masters, 2016).

Together, our stories and human experiences provide a window into the mystery of a creative God and insight into the capacity of all human beings to relate to one another, but most of all they help us to understand the importance of communication and communion.

Jesus: the model carer

Take thirty minutes, either alone or with others, and using the pointers in the box below, to consider the tools and methods that Jesus used to ensure that all people, regardless of their ability, were able to express their story and enter into a relationship with God.

Jesus cared!

1. When Jesus meets people, how does he model care that attends to people's stories?

2. Who was welcome within his ministry?

3. What do you think people experienced when Jesus spent time with them?

4. How did Jesus use creativity to remove barriers and invite people into a personal encounter with himself and the Father?

Jesus did not reject – indeed, he assigned dignity and importance to the very people society and the religious leaders rejected:

- He sought to meet the person before the disability or life situation. This was on offer to everyone, no matter what their ability was.

- He was "God's self-communication to humanity" (Masson, 1984).

- He embraced people's stories and life situations, assuring them of their call into the mystery and love of the Father.

- He ensured that everyone had access to his words, actions, ministry and mission and that not a single person was excluded.

- Jesus is God's revelation, human and divine united and walking among us (John 1:14: "And the Word became flesh and lived among us").

- He broke down barriers and showed that God's promise of belonging was real and for everyBody: he was our God and we his people (Exodus 6:7: "I will take you as my people, and I will be your God").

Spirituality: in the presence of God, experience and expression

Let us now turn to the area of spirituality (Tobanelli, 2010) and why it is an important area to be acknowledged and addressed in the lives of people who have been intellectually disabled.

Following the model of Christ, we are invited to meet the person where they are and for who they are: mind, body and spirit.

In the provision of care and in faith communities, we are legally required to consider and meet the spiritual needs of people who use our services – but what does spirituality mean? Is it just about going to church or about practising our faith?

Creative conversations and interaction with people who have been intellectually disabled has revealed a definition of spirituality that has relationship at its core.

Through hospitable structures and creative conversations, people with intellectual disabilities have begun to express their spiritual experiences. Their stories have shown that they do not feel their spirit to be detached from their material world and bodily experience: it is connected to them in every way.

The more conversations that take place, the more self-awareness develops. As people experience their inner self, they feel increasingly impelled to narrate their story and experience of God to others. Together people have started to enjoy mutual experiences and self-knowledge. This is a cyclical journey that begins with the self and "re-turns to the self" (Gangemi et al., 2010), during which the person is invited on a journey of exploration, as shown in the following diagram:

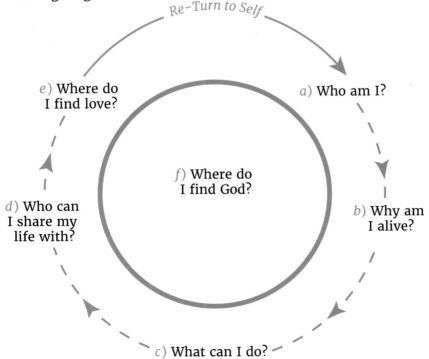

Re-Turn to Self

e) Where do I find love?

a) Who am I?

f) Where do I find God?

d) Who can I share my life with?

b) Why am I alive?

c) What can I do?

As each part of a person's life is creatively experienced and expressed, intellectual barriers fall away and people of all abilities are invited time and time again to name and notice things about themselves and their lives. By noticing such issues and reflecting upon God's presence, new knowledge occurs: we are invited to return to our self, having expressed our experience of God with new knowledge and purpose. We come to know that we matter!

Like Jesus, if we *deliberately* remove barriers obstructing the lives of people who have been disabled, a creative space will be available for spiritual expression. People of all abilities are drawn into relationships with others and with God, relationships marked by a profound sense of communion. When we are present and attentive to the other, a reciprocal exchange enables an authentic encounter (Gangemi et al., 2010). Is this not what Jesus did – remove barriers and avoid the danger of telling a person's story for them? Did Jesus not create empathic spaces where God could meet us *all* and where we could *all* meet God (based on *Dei Verbum*)? Such a model of care could go some way towards addressing the problems of isolation and loneliness.

Caring for the body, mind and spirit: a whole-person approach (see Gangemi, 2016a)

"To care and create space for spiritual expression is not, therefore, 'a moral task' that we are asked to make; rather, as we have explored, it is a human action which calls all people involved to be 'overwhelmingly attuned to human beings'."

Reinders, 2015, p. 363

Returning to the research project "EveryBody Has a Story", some confusion seemed to arise within the care and lives of people who have been intellectually disabled, one which prevented the expression of personal spirituality and faith.

In some faith communities, it seemed that people did not always know how to make all that they do accessible to people who need faith-based activities that are creative and accessible. This appeared to be challenging for some communities who were, more often than not, reliant on the written word.

At the same time, there has been a huge emphasis on the development of awareness, educational methods and approaches to communication within the lives and care of people with disabilities. This has been marked by an increase in creativity and an *enablement* of people who have been disabled. Modern technology, legislation, person-centred awareness of disability issues and symbolic forms of communication have made it possible for both Church and society to embrace the stories and expressions of intellectually disabled people. As a result, some barriers have begun to be removed and replaced with unprecedented possibilities.

> "Knowing why but not how;
> knowing how but not why"
>
> *EveryBody Has a Story",*
> *Gangemi et al., 2010*

The confusing situation therefore arises whereby there may be

> "people in faith communities who *know why* story-based care and spirituality is important, but may *not know how* to use the creative tools that are needed to accompany in a way that is enabling".
>
> *Gangemi et al., 2010*

On the other hand, due to new communication skills developed in some care services, there are carers who *know how* to remove barriers to creative learning but *not why* spirituality and story is important. This sets up a confusing barrier that can only be removed when a community makes a conscious commitment to *knowing how and why* barriers must be replaced with creative relationships.

A creative possibility

We have so far reflected upon how relationship, presence and the gift of friendship are slowly becoming a creative possibility. However, we have also discovered that there is still a long way to go before people "living with a disability (along with their families and carers) can feel as though they belong in a faith community" (Duke, 2016b).

The exciting thought is that, as a generation of Christians, we are each and every one of us called to discover the mysterious gift of life and of individual vocation.

Disabled people, as is true of all people, have an important part to play in God's plan of salvation. Activating this "ordinary" place of reflection on disability in the Church (Romero, 2016, p. 204) will require *all* people to enter into the mystery and sharing of authentic and respectful love. This *will* happen ordinarily through the gradual discovery of new and creative ways of *being together* as the Body of Christ.

How easy, amazing and authentic this new journey will be in a Church that is enriched with a symbolic tradition and call to love of one's neighbour!

So as to accompany you, the readers and the Church, in this journey of mutual discovery, we would like to give you some basic tools which we hope will *en*-able people of all abilities as they share their lives, stories and faith.

Jonathan's unique vision

In one parish where Cristina worked, she accompanied a family whose son was a creative learner and who was on the spectrum of autism.

Jonathan, a vibrant young man, was always keen to go to church, pulling at his mother's hand so that they were not late.

When Cristina was preparing the catechists for his First Communion, she began by meeting Jonathan and his family. She invited the catechists to ask Jonathan and his mum why he liked church so much. The answer came back "I like the colours, the priest and the smells."

His mother described the comforting effect on her son of the routine of the Mass but said that because people did not like the way in which he vocalised his joy, (he would creatively make a low-pitched sound) they usually sat at the back of the church in case they needed to make a quick exit.

While they belonged to the parish it seems they were not fully welcome. Because of this, although Jonathan wanted to go to church, his mum decided to stay away from Mass, unwilling to "upset" anyone.

As time passed, Jonathan's requests to return to church became too much to refuse and they began, once again, to attend – but also to sit in the back seats.

As we began to prepare for his First Communion, his mum phoned to ask what she could bring to the meeting following their prolonged absence from church.

Jonathan was a very skilled artist whose drawings transformed his daily experiences into diagrams that helped him process and remember what he did and saw. Like Jesus, he learnt and taught through actions and images. People on the spectrum of autism have a very literal and ordered experience of the world, and so Cristina suggested that Jonathan's mother should ask him to draw what he saw when he came to church.

When his mum came to Cristina with the picture she was completely humbled and stopped in her tracks.

Jonathan had drawn the moment when the priest lifts up the small white circle of the Eucharistic Bread for all to venerate – and there were stars and stripes radiating from it.

Cristina reflected that we had thought that we were preparing Jonathan to receive the Eucharist – yet his longing and creative drawing showed us something of the very grace of God. He had had no formal preparation as yet, had learned no Eucharistic vocabulary – and yet he "saw" the mystery of the body of Christ and the way in which it flows into our space and time.

Jonathan was our catechist, his creative way of learning akin to the very revelation of God.

6

Guidelines for knowing "how" and "why"

Please take one or two hours for the following exercise.
You can organise your own time to reflect alone or in a group:

Using the guidelines to know "how" and "why":

1. Please read through James and Susanna's story below.
   Note what strikes you about each person.

2. Make a list of James' skills and a list of his needs.

3. What do you think you would need to know about James?

4. How could you ensure that James can experience "belonging"
   in your care services, activities or ministry?

Make notes/list "what I need to know and have":

5. Now read through the guidelines. Please make notes of anything
   new that strikes you/list "what you need to know and have"
   if you are to enable stories.

6. How could you ensure that James can share his story and enjoy
   a true sense of belonging within your care/ministry/services?

7. What opportunities could you create to ensure that James and
   Susanna avoid loneliness?

James and Susanna's story

James is a vibrant young man of twenty-two who loves to live and to practise his faith. James has a close relationship with his family but has recently moved into his own home. He is enjoying living independently and making choices for himself, but he misses his parents and siblings. He meets his family every Sunday at church. On one particular Sunday, he invites another person, Susanna, who lives with him, to join him for church. After two months, Susanna shares with James that she wants to be baptised. James' family ask you for help. James has Down syndrome and Susanna is non-verbal, a creative learner who lives on the spectrum of autism.

Read through the guidelines below and decide *what you would do next.*

Some tips for discerning needs/knowing "how" and "why"

Each person is an individual whose skills and needs will be as unique as they are. Their story is important. As the Image of God, each person reflects God into the world and the Church. As such, space and activities must be created for people to narrate their story and have their needs met within a culture of respect-filled belonging.

People with intellectual disabilities often process information at a slow pace, needing time, symbols and objects to make links and enjoy communication.

The environment in which you share should not be overrun with sensory, audio and visual clutter as this may lead to overstimulation, causing anxiety and challenges to the emotional state of people with intellectual disabilities. This can sometimes present in varying types of behaviour.

Make sure that you communicate in an empathic way, one which *en*-ables the skills of the person. This will ensure that triggers to anxieties and behaviours are not set off and the experience becomes a mutual space to *be together within each other's story.*

To be sure that you do not put in place inaccessible intellectual boundaries, here are some tips to set you in the right direction for easy access and story sharing:

- Keep your language free from jargon and complicated words.

- Use plain English and keep your sentences simple.

- Make sure that your sentences and questions are within the other person's experience.

- Get to know each other and try and discern exactly what the other person's needs are and how they process language.

- You can use the following ASPE (Aim, Structure, Process, Experience) process to help you develop language and ask questions (Gangemi et al., 2010).

It will be important to watch the person with whom you wish to communicate and begin to understand the way in which they actually communicate and the skills and tools which they use and may need.

A: Aim of the question: What is the purpose of asking this question? What does it aim to discover or reveal? What is the area of people's lives we want to explore, and why?

S: Structure of the question: How is the question structured? What words are used? What are the key elements of the question? What is the level of complexity and the type of answer required?

P: Process: Will the person be able to process the question effectively? What will their cognitive response to the question be and what will they understand?

E: Experience of participants: Is the question within the life or faith experience of the person?

Once this is established, there are some basic questions you should answer:

Choice

What choice-making skills does the person enjoy? Could symbols or visual objects aid this process?

Assertiveness

Can the person initiate, question, disagree and control activities? Will symbols or objects aid this by providing a symbolic or visual reference to assist communication, understanding and experience?

Questions

Can the person ask questions? How do they ask? Could symbols or objects help in forming structures for questions to be asked and answered? Will symbols or objects help to prompt and assist memory and attention?

Friendship

What are the person's language skills? What opportunities does he/she have to meet and make friends? What time do they have to share with friends? How does he/she interact and do they need help with this skill? Could symbols promote interaction, language skills or social skills? Can he/she have an intimate conversation with a friend or family member?

Independence and learning skills

What are the person's independence skills? Does the person need sensory aids to be independent? Who could be her/his hands, ears, and eyes? How could dignity and independence be maintained? Are you visible to the person with disability? Are you too close, too far away from the focus point at prayer time?

Physical access

Is there sufficient space for someone in their wheelchair to move freely or be helped? Is the wheelchair in a good position in group activities? Is there a loop system? Do people have clear access to lip reading? Do you need sign language skills? How can you find out?

Sensory skills and needs

Does the person respond to touch? Is touch immediately personally challenging? How could this be overcome if they are to respond and build relationships? Once relationship and trust is established, how can you move forward?

Always focus on what *can* be done, not on what *cannot*.

Sarah, holiness and beauty

The potential of each person, found so clearly in the promise of God, was brought home to us very powerfully by an insight from Sarah, one of the young women in the "EveryBody Has a Story" project.

Sarah was a very wonderful young woman with Down Syndrome. Like Moses, she spoke slowly with a tremor, which caused her to choose not to vocalise. We found, however, that by using creative methods for communication and an empathic approach she began to share her thoughts. Her insight became one of the most profound expressions of a call to holiness.

When asking Sarah to explain the word "holy", she told us in a low but deliberate voice that it was "as if people were beautiful".

Sarah was a creative learner and a careful teacher. Her answer was not related to God but to the potential in human nature.

These realities of being special and beautiful are assigned to all people, for everyone is called to holiness. Sarah's insight liberated people from disabling labels and situated these same individuals within God's call to holiness.

This liberation and call is powerfully shared in God's invitation and self-revelation to Moses, called to liberate God's people and to foster communities of belonging. As he did with Moses, God entrusted Sarah to reveal something of herself to others.

Using symbols, movement and visual aids in care and prayer

The Christian tradition has always relied upon symbols, actions, images and vibrant colours. If we carefully observe our liturgies we can notice that they are rich in rituals and movement.

In the Eucharist, we remember Christ. We participate with our brothers and sisters in the Lord's own sacrifice, and through our receiving of Jesus in the Eucharist, we are brought more fully into communion with him and with each other. In our Eucharistic celebration, we spend time with Christ and with each other and encounter Christ and our brothers and sisters at a deep level. A whole range of symbols, images, objects and sounds are used. The beautiful movements that surround the sacrament of the Eucharist speak to the heart. These sounds and symbols speak to all of us, including to our brothers and sisters with intellectual disabilities – our creative learners – who can respond to these beautiful movements.

Vibrant colours, candles, familiar objects, repetitive music (that is not too challenging or complicated), as well as textured and multi-coloured materials, are all useful when planning for story gathering or times of prayer.

For example:

When sharing about God and prayer with a person who does not use words and who experiences profound intellectual disabilities, you could do the following:

1. Create a beautiful prayer space which appeals to the senses, place a picture of Jesus on the focal point and carefully use electric decorative light strings.

2. Using a piece of material that is soft and (safely) warmed, invite the person to hold the material, maybe to touch their face with it.

3. Ask them to show how it feels, maybe by smiling or using facial expressions. Observe how they respond.

4. Share how "God's love may feel soft as we pray" – "We feel God, we feel the material."

5. Using song, pictures or words, share that "Jesus' love is soft and warm". This should make a link and create a prayerful experience.

6. Using your focal point (see point 1 above), invite the person to express what is happening. Ask them to show how God's love feels. Have some resources to choose from. Leave space and time for the person to creatively express themselves. These are sacramental moments of true presence, of God-communication, of the Re–Turn to the self and an opportunity for God's grace to be experienced.

- It is important never to assume that the individual with whom you are sharing faith has no understanding. Always speak directly to the person with a disability.

- Make decisions together, for each person is valuable and has a vital contribution to make in life and in faith.

- Be creative together, inventing new ways to differentiate so that noBody feels different or left out.

- Never work from a culture of "them and us", but instead operate within an environment of communion and hope.

Prayerful action

This activity aims to help you to foster communities of belonging in your church and life. Please recruit two people who can help you.

We exist together and are held in that mysterious truth that relationship and friendship bring about the authentic and loving presence of God.

A deeper exploration of disability, mystery and community, within the human and Christian story, will lead us on a journey of mutual discovery and towards the realisation of the awesomeness of God's creative actions.

This is summed up well in an insight from Sarah Long, a theologian with a disability: "This is me," Sarah shares. "I belong: accept me as I am. This is my God who understands me, befriends me and guides me. I am his reflection" (Long, 2016, p. 193).

As we come towards the end of this journey of reflection into the lives and care of people who have been disabled, take five minutes and ask yourself:

1. What, now, are the first images and words that come to my mind when I see or hear the following word?

   Disability

2. Write down or record your reactions.

3. What do you notice has changed from your list, made at the start of the journey?

7

Creative prayer

As we come to the end of this book, may we extend our last invitation to active and creative prayer?

Creative prayer with Psalm 139 (vv1–4, 13–15)

O LORD, you have searched me and known me.
You know when I sit down and when I rise up;
you discern my thoughts from far away.
You search out my path and my lying down,
and are acquainted with all my ways.
Even before a word is on my tongue,
O Lord, you know it completely
...

For it was you who formed my inward parts;
 you knit me together in my mother's womb.
I praise you, for I am fearfully and wonderfully made.
 Wonderful are your works;
that I know very well.
My frame was not hidden from you,
when I was being made in secret,
 intricately woven in the depths of the earth.

The welcome

Recruit two to four volunteers. Gather as a group of friends who wish to pray and make a difference in the lives of people with intellectual disabilities or people who may be lonely.

Invite people who have been disabled to join you for a meal.

Before you meet, please take some time to simplify the language of the psalm above, so that it can be accessible to a creative learner.

Once you have done this, plan some time to eat and pray together:

The invitation

Invite people of mixed abilities to join you for a creative prayer time and for a meal. You might like to use some images to help understand the words.

Person 1: Pray the words of the psalm aloud. (This can be done through sign, BSL or word, according to needs.)

All: Listen or watch.

All: Reflect in silence for three minutes, noting what struck you.

Person 2: Pray the words of the psalm aloud. (This can be done through sign, BSL or word, according to needs.)

All: Listen or watch.

All: Reflect in silence for two minutes, noting what struck you.

Please share what struck you with others.

Using the guidelines, help people to share in a way that celebrates their communication skills. Note down the insights that emerge.

You may like to have a basket to gather these insights.

Together, make a poster/drama/story bag/story book that shows what has struck you or create a drama that can be shared. When this is done, share a meal together.

The Image of God

Find a creative way to share the insights, prayers and images that have emerged from your time together. Share them with your parish, family and friends and, if possible, with your local community. Be the Image of God in the world.

A prayer for you to recite and reflect upon alone or in a group:

Father, Son and Holy Spirit,

may we be the image of your creative love in the world.

May we build communities where all people belong.

Be always at our side.

Be always in our actions.

For when we have you, we have all things.

Conclusion

The reflections contained in this short book are designed to prompt us to consider why and how our brothers and sisters with intellectual disabilities are cared for.

An initial reflection on the language that is used in discussion about disability generally reminds us of how this shapes our understanding of the personhood of people with disabilities, which in turn has consequences for the way we care.

Some activities are included which provide a framework for a discussion to take place around the language that is used when we speak about people with intellectual disabilities.

In terms of how we care for people with disabilities, various models and approaches are available to us. An outmoded medical model of disability has given way to the social model of disability, and while much valuable progress has been made in making lives better as a result, more deliberate attention must be paid to how the lives and stories of people with disabilities can be celebrated as an ordinary way of being human.

The problems of isolation and loneliness which are a sad reality for many in our society, including our brothers and sisters with intellectual disabilities, are an example of what can happen when we fail to care.

In turning to Christian theology and its understanding of "communion" as expressed in the Christian practices of friendship and hospitality, the solution to loneliness appears in the faithful practice of these principles.

One way of demonstrating our friendship and hospitality, and of showing that we do care, is through gathering, interpreting, sharing and celebrating the stories of people with intellectual disabilities. Stories, the telling of which allows us in turn to share our stories, thereby foster the kind of life-giving relationships that allow every one of us to live life in all its fullness. The reality that "everyBody has a story" reminds us that stories are to be shared, and that when they are shared, they have the power to transform both the storyteller and the listener.

While much great caring work is being done in churches and parishes with people who have disabilities, much remains to be done before our communities are authentic places of belonging for all people.

With this in mind, we hope that this resource will help others to carefully consider why we care and to see that when we do care, we are living as God intended us to live.

Bibliography

Badetti, L. (2016) Self and Community: The Importance of Interdependence and its Shadow Side, *Journal of Disability* and Religion, vol 20(3), pp. 154-162.

Bennett, J. (2013) Chapter 12: Women, Disabled. In J. Swinton and B. Brock (Eds), *Disability in the Christian Tradition.* Grand Rapids, MI/Cambridge: Wm. B. Eerdmans.

Bigby, C. (2004) *Ageing with a Lifelong Disability: A Guide to Practice, Programme and Policy Issues for Human Services Professionals.* London: Jessica Kingsley Publishers.

Blackman, N. (2003) *Loss and Learning Disability.* London: Worth Publishing.

Cacioppo, John T. and Patrick, William (2008) *Loneliness: Human Nature and the Need for Social Connection.* New York: W.W. Norton and Company.

Duke, Z. (2016) From Inclusion to Belonging: Navigating a Way Forward. Disability, Culture and Faith: a celebration paper delivered at LUMSA University, Rome, 23-26 June 2016. Available from Zachariah Duke, Zachariah.Duke@uon.edu.au

Duke, Z. and Vanier (2017) *A Witness to God's Peace: A Jean Vanier Symposium* https://www.bbi.catholic.edu.au/news-events/fx-events.cfm?loadref=111&id= 201&seftoken=jean-vanier-exclusive-screening/685

Flannery, O.P. (Ed.) (1998) *Vatican Council II. Vol. 1: The Conciliar and Post Conciliar Documents.* New York: Costello Publishing.

Gangemi, C. (2016a) Are Our Communities a Place of Belonging? https:// www.livability.org.uk/communities-place-belonging-working-partnership-inclusion/

Gangemi, C. (2016b) *Culture e Fede Special,* vol. XXIV, Introduction. Available from cgangemi.kairos@gmail.com

Gangemi, C., Tobanelli, M., Vincenzi, G. and Swinton, J. (2010) "EveryBody Has a Story." Published research report, University of Aberdeen. Available from cgangemi.kairos@gmail.com

Gillibrand, J. (2010) *Disabled Church – Disabled Society: The Implications of Autism for Philosophy, Theology and Politics.* London: Jessica Kingsley Publishers.

Henley, C. (2016) *Culture e Fede Special,* vol. XXIV, Chapter 9. Available from cgangemi.kairos@gmail.com

Hogan, R. (2006) *The Theology of the Body in John Paul II.* Frederick, MD: The Word Among Us Press.

Jones, D. (2004) *Soul of the Embryo: Christianity and the Human Embryo.* London: A&C Black.

Kugler, S. (2013) Chaplaincy in a Changing World. In L. Forster-Smith (Ed.), *College and University Chaplaincy in the 21st Century: A Multi-Faith Look at the Practice of Ministry on Campuses across America.* Nashville: Skylight Paths.

Livability (2017) www.livability.org.uk/share-story-listening-service-users/

Long, S. (2016) *Culture e Fede Special,* vol. XXIV, Chapter 6. Available from cgangemi.kairos@gmail.com

Masson, R. (1984) Spirituality for the Head, Heart, Hands and Feet: An Approach to the First Course. e-Publications@Marquette

Masters, A. (2016) *Culture e Fede Special,* vol. XXIV, Chapter 5. Available from cgangemi.kairos@gmail.com

Matthews, P. (2013) *Pope John Paul II and the Apparently Non-Acting Person.* Leominster: Gracewing.

Matthews, P. (2016) *Culture e Fede Special,* vol XXIV, Chapter 4. Available from cgangemi.kairos@gmail.com

Mencap (2016) Friendship and Socialising: Research and Statistics. [online]. Available from: https://www.mencap.org.uk/learning-disability-explained/research-and-statistics/friendships-and-socialising-research-and (accessed 5 October 2017).

Moltmann, J. (1974) *Man: Christian Anthropology in the Conflicts of the Present,* trans. John Sturdy. London: SPCK.

Pope Francis (2016) Address of His Holiness Pope Francis to Participants in the Convention for Persons with Disabilities Promoted by the Italian Episcopal Conference. June. http://bit.ly/2yHRQBY

Reinders, H.S. (2008) *Receiving the Gift of Friendship*. Grand Rapids, MI: Wm. B. Eerdmans.

Reinders, H.S. (2015) Religious Perspectives, Transforming Friendship: An Essay in Honor of Jean Vanier, *Journal of Religion, Disability & Health*, vol. 19, pp. 340-364. DOI 10.1080/23312521.2015.1093903

Reinders, H.S. (2016) *Culture e Fede Special*, vol. XXIV, Chapter 3. Available from cgangemi.kairos@gmail.com

Reinders, J. (2016) "Seeing with the Eyes of God." Symposium introduction, in Living Fully Statement, 23 June 2016 (see www.livingfully2016.com).

Romero, M. (2016) *Culture e Fede Special*, vol. XXIV, Chapter 10. Available from cgangemi.kairos@gmail.com

Second Vatican Council (1965) *Dei Verbum*: Dogmatic Constitution on Divine Revelation.

Swinton, J. (2001) Building a Church for Strangers, *Journal of Religion, Disability & Health*, vol. 4(4). https://www.abdn.ac.uk/sdhp/documents/buildingachurchforstrangers.pdf

Swinton, John (2010) Disability Theology. In Ian McFarland, David Fergusson, Karen Kilby and Iain Torrance (Eds), *Cambridge Dictionary of Christian Theology*. London: Cambridge University Press.

Tanner, K. (1993) The Difference Theological Anthropology Makes, *Theology Today*, vol. 50(4), pp. 567-579.

Tobanelli, M. (2010) Unpublished research paper presented at "EveryBody Has a Story" launch, London. Available from cgangemi.kairos@gmail.com

Vanier, J. (1989) *Community and Growth*, rev. ed. New York: Paulist Press.

Volf, M. (2002) Theology for a Way of Life. In M. Volf and D.C. Bass (Eds), *Practicing Theology: Beliefs and Practices in the Christian Life*, pp. 245-263. Grand Rapids, MI: Wm. B. Eerdmans.

Waldron, L. (2016) *Culture e Fede Special*, vol. XXIV, Chapter 7. Available from cgangemi.kairos@gmail.com